Why Why Why do people want to explore?

MiLes
KeLLy
PUBLISHING

First published in 2005 by
Miles Kelly Publishing Ltd
Bardfield Centre, Great Bardfield, Essex, CM7 4SL

Copyright © Miles Kelly Publishing Ltd 2005

2 4 6 8 10 9 7 5 3 1

Editorial Director
Belinda Gallagher

Art Director
Jo Brewer

Assistant Editor
Lucy Dowling

Volume Designer
Sally Lace

Indexer
Hilary Bird

Production Manager
Elizabeth Brunwin

Reprographics
Anthony Cambray, Liberty Newton, Ian Paulyn

ISBN 978-1-84236-907-4

Printed in China

British Library Cataloguing-in-Publication Data
A catalogue record for this book is available
from the British Library

www.mileskelly.net
info@mileskelly.net

Contents

Who wanted to find a magical land?

In ancient times, Egyptian queen Hatshepsut sent explorers to look for a magical land. The land, called Punt, was full of treasure and beautiful animals. Hatshepsut's sailors brought back gold, ivory, monkeys and perfumes for the queen.

Queen Hatshepsut

Flat world!

The ancient Egyptians thought the world was flat and rectangular, with the sea running around the edge.

Who crossed the Alps with elephants?

In 22 BC Hannibal Barca, a famous military leader, invaded Italy. To get to Rome, and avoid being attacked, he took 46,000 soldiers and 37 war elephants across the Alps. It was one of the greatest military operations ever carried out in ancient times.

Make
Draw a map of your own magical land and colour it in. Don't forget to name it.

Hannibal

Who were the best sailors?

The best sailors in ancient times were the Phoenicians (say 'fuh-nee-shuns'). They came from what is now Syria and Lebanon and sailed all over the Mediterranean Sea. The Phoenicians used ships that had sails and oars.

Who was Marco Polo?

Marco Polo was a famous explorer who lived in Italy in the 1200s. He travelled to Asia at a time when most people in Europe never went far from their homes. Altogether, Marco travelled over 40,000 kilometres.

Marco Polo

Think

Imagine that you are a famous explorer. Write a list of everything you would need to take on your travels.

What did Marco Polo discover?

Marco Polo discovered lots of amazing inventions on his travels through Asia. He saw fireworks, paper money, ice-cream and eyeglasses for the first time. He also discovered that the Chinese had a postage system and could post each other letters.

Empty deserts!

On the way to China, Marco Polo crossed the vast, empty Desert of Lop, now called the Gobi Desert.

Who searched for a gold city?

In the 1500s, Spanish explorers searched for a mysterious city called El Dorado. Everything in the city was said to be made of gold. However, they never found the city, and people believed that the gold had been melted down and sent abroad.

Which explorer was very unlucky?

In the 1300s, Moroccan explorer Ibn Battuta, dreamt that a giant bird picked him up and carried him away. Battuta thought that the dream was a sign from God, telling him to go exploring. During his travels he did not have much luck. He was kept prisoner, chased by pirates, attacked by thieves and shipwrecked.

Ibn Battuta

Why did explorers travel in junk?

A junk was a giant Chinese sailing ship. In ancient times, Zheng He, a Chinese explorer, had the largest sailing junks on Earth. The biggest was 130 metres long and 60 metres wide.

Discover

Where did you last go on holiday? How did you get there? How long did it take you?

Who was not allowed to explore?

Xuan-Zang, an ancient explorer, was banned from exploring by the Chinese emperor. He sneaked out of China and returned 16 years later with holy books and statues. The emperor was so pleased, he gave him a royal welcome.

Family values!

In many of the places Ibn Battuta visited, he got married. He had several wives and children in different parts of the world!

Who brought back a giraffe?

The Chinese sailor, Zheng He Zheng, was one of the world's best explorers. In the 1400s, he sailed to Africa. On his travels he collected precious stones, plants and animals to take back to the emperor. The emperor's favourite present was a giraffe from east Africa.

Zheng He Zheng

Star sailing!

Before the compass was invented, the first explorers had to rely on their observations of the Moon and stars to find their way.

Vasco da Gama

Who found the route to Asia?

In the 1400s, Portugese sailor Vasco da Gama sailed to Calicut in India to find spices. The rajah, Calicut's ruler, did not let da Gama take any spices, so he went home empty-handed. However, the King of Portugal was very happy that da Gama had found the sea route to Asia.

Why were spices like gold?

In the 1400s, spices such as cinnamon and nutmeg were as valuable as gold. Spices came from Asia and were carried to Europe on the backs of camels. This took a long time and made them very expensive to buy.

Who found the Americas?

Christopher Columbus found the Americas by mistake! He wanted to sail around the world to Asia in his ship the *Santa Maria*. When Columbus spotted land in 1492, he thought he had sailed to Japan. In fact, he had found the Bahamas, just off the American mainland.

Santa Maria →

Discover

Which sea is closest to where you live? Look in an atlas or on a map to find out.

Why did Columbus make a mistake?

Christopher Columbus

Because he had travelled to the wrong place! As Columbus thought he had arrived in Asia, he called the lands he found the West Indies, and the people he met, Indians. They are still called this today – even though the West Indies are thousands of miles from India.

Hot stuff!

Sailors were afraid to sail around Africa. This was because of a myth that said if people went too far south in the Atlantic Ocean, the Sun would burn them to ashes.

Where was Vinland?

Five hundred years before Columbus, the Vikings found a new land and called it Vinland. They left after they kept getting into fights with the local people. Today, Vinland is known as America.

Who played a nasty trick?

The Spanish explorer Francisco Pizarro captured the Inca leader Atahuallpa in 1532. Atahuallpa said that if Pizarro set him free, he would give him a room filled with gold. Pizarro agreed. Once Atahuallpa had handed over the gold, Pizarro killed him and took over the Inca capital city, Cuzco.

Francisco Pizarro

Why did a dog get paid?

Spanish explorer Vasco Nuñez de Balboa sailed to America in 1500 looking for treasure. He took his beloved dog, Leoncico, with him. Leoncico never left his master's side and Balboa even paid him his own wage.

Whale of a time!

When sailing past Scotland, Greek explorer Pytheas was amazed to see fish as big as boats. In fact they weren't fish – they were whales.

Vasco Nuñez de Balboa

How did explorers tell the time?

Explorers could not tell the time at sea because clocks didn't work on ships. John Harrison, an inventor, created a new clock (called the chronometer) that could measure the time precisely, even at sea.

Look

Next time you go on a journey, write down how many different kinds of animals you see.

Which city was hiding?

 **In the 1400s, the Inca people of South America built a city called Machu Picchu on top of a mountain.** Built from large stones and watered by a spring at the top of the mountain, the city was so well-hidden, that Spanish invaders never found it. An American explorer re-discovered the city in 1911.

Machu Picchu

Play

With your friends, play a game of hide and seek. Take it in turns to be the hider and the seeker.

Who founded the New World?

In 1607, 100 British people arrived in what is now called the United States of America. They founded the first permanent settlement and others soon followed. The continent was named the New World, and Europe, Asia and Africa became known as the Old World.

Ferdinand Magellan

Rich pickings!

In the 1500s, Francis Drake captured a Spanish treasure ship. It was carrying a cargo that was worth more than £12 million in today's money.

Who tried to sail around the world?

Portuguese explorer, Ferdinand Magellan, wanted to sail around the world during the 1500s. Magellan thought he could get to Asia and buy spices. Many of his crew died from a disease called scurvy and Magellan himself was killed in war. Only one of his five ships sailed home safely.

Who went on an important mission?

In 1768, Captain James Cook was sent on an important mission by the British navy. He went to the island of Tahiti and made observations of the planet Venus passing in front of the Sun. He also explored Australia, New Zealand and the Pacific Islands and made new maps.

What was scurvy?

Scurvy is a serious disease that is caused by not eating enough fresh fruit and vegetables. Many explorers and sailors suffered from the disease when on long voyages, as they had no access to fruit and vegetables.

Dr Livingstone

Captain Cook

Which explorer went missing?

In 1869, the explorer Dr Livingstone went missing. He'd gone exploring in east Africa and no one had heard from him. Everyone thought he had died. An American writer, Henry Stanley, found him in Tanzania. He greeted him with the words, "Dr Livingstone, I presume?"

Tasty trip!

Captain Cook was the first European to discover Hawaii, in 1778. He called it the Sandwich Island.

Who first crossed America?

Meriwether Lewis and William Clark travelled across America in 1803.

They sailed down rivers on a boat. When the rivers grew too narrow, Lewis and Clark used canoes. Local Native American guides helped them paddle their canoe and find their way across America.

Lewis and Clark

Brotherly love!

Lewis and Clark met some fierce native warriors whilst exploring. By amazing chance, the warrior leader turned out to be the brother of their guide.

Who went exploring in disguise?

The French explorer Rene Caillie wanted to visit the ancient city of Timbuktu, but only Muslims were allowed in. He dressed up as an Arab trader and sneaked into the city in 1828. He was the first European to go there and return home alive.

Rene Caillie

Make it

Create a disguise for yourself using hats, sunglasses and old clothes. Does anyone recognize you?

Who was scared by bears?

American explorer Meriwether Lewis was chased by a bear whilst out hunting. Lewis tried to shoot the bear, but he ran out of bullets. The bear chased Lewis into a river, then walked away and left him alone.

Who tried to get to the North Pole?

Norwegian explorer, Fridtjof Nansen did. He built a ship called *Fram*, which was designed to get stuck in the ice without being damaged. It was the strongest wooden ship of its time. As the iced moved, it carried the *Fram* nearer to the North Pole. Nansen almost reached the Pole in 1895, but not quite.

Pole position!

In 1911, the explorer Roald Amundsen and his team were the first people to reach the South Pole.

Who crossed Australia?

The middle of Australia is so hot, it is very hard to travel across. In 1860, Robert Burke and William Wills entered a competition set by the government to cross the middle of Australia. Both explorers starved to death and only one member of their team survived.

Burke and Wills

Who were the first Australians?

Aborigines were the first people to live in Australia. They arrived from Asia over 70,000 years ago. Many Aborigines lived in the Australian outback. Here, it is very hot and dry, and a long way from any big towns.

The Fram

Discover

Write a list of all the different animals you would expect to find in Australia.

Did explorers travel by sled?

In 1910, an explorer called Roald Amundsen used dog sleds to travel to the South Pole. Husky dogs pulled the sleds, and if a dog died, it was fed to the other dogs. This reduced the amount of food the men had to carry. Amundsen reached the South Pole in 1911.

Roald Amundsen and his team

Who conquered Everest?

On 29 May, 1953, Tenzing and Hillary, were the first people to reach the top of Mount Everest, the highest mountain in the world. Since then, many other people have climbed the mountain.

Think

What sports can you play in the ice and snow? Have you tried doing any?

Peary and Henson

How did explorers keep warm at the North Pole?

By wearing sealskins! American explorer Robert Peary and his assistant Matthew Henson wore sealskin clothes when they travelled to the North Pole in 1909. The skins were light, waterproof and very warm. Peary paid local people to make his clothes and equipment.

A mountain of rubbish!

Today Mount Everest is covered in litter and old oxygen tanks left behind by climbers.

Who explored the natural world?

Charles Darwin went on a round-the-world voyage on a ship called the *Beagle*. Darwin was a nature expert and found many new birds, plants, insects and other living things. Once back in England, Darwin wrote important books about the natural world.

Who discovered nine cities?

In 1870, a German called Heinrich Schliemann travelled to Turkey to see if he could find the ancient city of Troy. He discovered the ruins of nine cities, and also dug up piles of beautiful gold jewellery.

Charles Darwin

Going ape!

In 1871, Darwin wrote a book called The Descent of Man. In the book, Darwin said that the very first humans were related to apes.

Which ship explored the seabed?

In 1872, a ship called HMS Challenger set out to explore a new world – the bottom of the sea. The ship measured the seabed, using ropes to find out the depth of the ocean. On its round-the-world voyage, Challenger's crew also found many new kinds of sea creatures.

Draw

You have discovered a new type animal. Draw a picture of it and give it a name.

HMS Challenger

How did people get to the Moon?

In 1969, astronauts travelled to the Moon in a spacecraft called *Apollo 11.* It was launched into space by a huge rocket. It took three days to get to the Moon. Once there, the astronauts spent two hours exploring before flying back to Earth.

Look

Can you see the Moon and stars when you look at the night sky?

Apollo 11

Space animals!

The first astronaut in space wasn't a human, but a dog named Laika. Sadly, Laika died during the voyage, but she led the way for more space exploration.

Who was the first man on the Moon?

The first person to stand on the Moon's surface was American astronaut Neil Armstrong, followed by Buzz Aldrin. They were part of the crew of *Apollo 11*. Both men collected rocks to take back to Earth.

Yuri Gagarin

Who was the first human in space?

In 1961, Yuri Gagarin became the first human to go into space. Gagarin flew around the Earth once in his spacecraft called *Vostok 1*. This took nearly two hours. He then travelled back to Earth and landed safely.

Quiz time

Do you remember what you have read about explorers? These questions will test your memory. The pictures will help you. If you get stuck, read the pages again.

3. Who brought back a giraffe?

page 10

4. Why were spices like gold?

page 11

page 7

1. Who searched for a gold city?

5. Who played a nasty trick?

page 14

page 8

2. Which explorer was very unlucky?

6. How did explorers tell the time?

page 15

page 18

11. Who conquered Everest?

page 25

7. Who went on an important mission?

8. Who was scared by bears?

page 21

12. Who explored the natural world?

page 26

9. Who tried to get to the North Pole?

page 22

13. Who was the first man on the Moon?

page 29

10. Who were the first Australians?

page 23

Index